The Lightworker's Compendium

Volume 1

Reiki Distance Healing Made Simple:
A no-symbols guide to offering powerful remote healing sessions

Manifesting Made Simple:
How to engage the Universe in bringing your best life into being

Who Are You, and Why Have You Become So Strange?
How to deal with questions from skeptics, naysayers, and ourselves when we become more intuitive,
spiritual, or both.

Alice Langholt, M.Msc.
Reiki Master Teacher

Copyright © 2017 Alice Langholt

All rights reserved. No reprints or reproduction of any part of this manual unless express permission by the author is obtained first. Author may be contacted via alicelangholt.com

ISBN-13: 978-1546473749
ISBN-10: 1546473742:

DEDICATION

I dedicate this work to all who are seeking, finding, and developing the Lightworker in themselves.

If your connection to something bigger guides you to influence your life and how you live, may you find the information here helpful in supporting your work.

I greet you, fellow Lightworker.
We are companions on this Journey. Namaste.

Alice Langholt

CONTENTS

Introduction	i
Reiki Distance Healing Made Simple	1
Manifesting Made Simple	63
Who Are You, and Why Have You Become So Strange?	107
About the Author	145

Alice Langholt

INTRODUCTION

In this Compendium, you will find three resources for your development and understanding of the essence of working with the Universe and Life Force Energy for healing, and for making your life better.

The first, *Reiki Distance Healing Made Simple*, explains in practical terms how to understand distance healing, many ways to do it, and how to know that it's working.

The second resource, *Manifesting Made Simple*, teaches you the essential ingredients in working with the Universe to bring your goals and dreams into being.

The third resource, *Who Are You, and Why Have You Become So Strange?* will help you understand when your growth separates you from others, and teaches you how to assess and adjust as needed.

We're evolving, and you are part of the new energy of our time. Embrace it, and know that you are supported. May these resources help you, and may the future volumes continue to enhance your growth.

If I can be of support to you in any way, please contact me via ReikiAwakening.com/contact. Thank you for reading, and thank you for being exactly who you are. You matter.

Alice Langholt

The Lightworker's Compendium V.1

Reiki Distance Healing Made Simple

A no-symbols guide to offering
powerful remote healing sessions

Alice Langholt, Reiki Master Teacher

Contents

Acknowledgments	4
Foreword	5
Introduction	8
How does Reiki Really Work?	11
How does Distance Healing Work?	16
What Distance Healing is and isn't	19
What About Symbols?	22
What a Practitioner and/or Recipient Might Feel During Distance Healing	27
What about Permission? Is that needed?	30
The Basic "Formula" for Sending Distance Reiki:	37
Scanning	38
Three ways to send distance Reiki relative to time	41
Ways to Strengthen Distance Healing Practice	47
Seven Techniques for Distance Healing	50

Volunteer Organizations Looking for Distance
Healers   55

Other Uses for Distance Healing   57

Excellent Reiki-Related Websites   59

Recommended Resources   61

Acknowledgements

I'd like to acknowledge the following people who helped me expand my horizons and grow into this amazing and beautiful skill, as well as one who is blessed to instruct others in doing the same:

Tamar Geri, who introduced me to Reiki

Ole Gabrielsen, whose Kundalini Reiki method showed me how to go beyond symbols.

Connie Dohan and Ernie Betz, who pushed me to take things farther.

Danene Legarth and Adina Bloom, who became my willing guinea pigs in my distance healing experiments.

Evan Langholt, who went from my skeptical challenger to being the one who brags about me.

My students, over a thousand, who constantly validate the results and power of this work.

Thank you all for your part in helping me discover who I am, and encouraging me to fearlessly push my own limits.

Foreword

Distance healing is not prayer. Prayer is asking a Higher Being to intervene and bring about a desired result.

It's also not magic. Magic implies that something is paranormal, or outside the realm of possibility for most people. But anyone who wishes to can learn to give distance healing.

Distance healing is a way of helping another living being receive additional life force energy, in order to bring himself into balance physically, emotionally, or spiritually. Life force energy is already a part of every living being. However, one's energy reserves can become blocked or depleted due to stress, illness, pain, or negative emotions. Offering distance healing to someone is like pouring a replenishing wellspring over him, so that he can take what is needed and apply it in the best way for his needs.

There are many energy healing methods, and most of them have some systems for doing distance healing. This book will assume that the reader has some familiarity with at least one of them. Reiki is the most commonly studied energy healing method. However, any practitioner of a method that includes working with life force energy in some way can benefit from learning these distance healing techniques and adding them to his or her practice.

What's Inside

This book includes simple and powerful techniques for effective distance healing, ways of understanding and developing intuition, and some anecdotes from my own practice. I will dispel myths about distance healing, and provide you with practical ways to start offering distance healing, and validating your practice. Experience is the best teacher, and getting feedback is the best way to grow confidence. The methods in this book will help you achieve success and confidence in your distance healing abilities.

Becoming a Powerful Distance Healer

As with most any skill, the person who puts in the right sort of practice will grow to be very good at distance healing. What does it mean to be good at distance healing? Perhaps the answer will surprise you.

Being good at distance healing doesn't mean that the recipient of the distance healing will always recover. It doesn't make you a "healer" or a "guru." It doesn't make you famous. Being good at distance healing means that you've learned to understand your intuitive signals well enough to really feel "connected" with the person (or plant or animal) to which you are sending distance healing. It means that you have attained a confidence, which comes from experience, that the energy work you are doing *does something*. Being good at distance healing means that, quite often, you are able to sense the places in your recipient that are out of balance. You may also receive other intuitive information about the person's physical or emotional health.

Here is the most important thing to know about distance healing: the results are not up to you. You are not a healer of another person. Offering distance healing places you in the role of **facilitator** of the recipient's healing. The recipient's Higher Self will apply the energy for his highest and best, which may or may not be what you had hoped it would do. In fact, your wishes for the energy are only requests. You are only a healer when you, yourself, heal. When your body heals itself, you are a healer. It simply is not correct to claim to be a healer of or for another person. The recipient's free will always rules.

Introduction

A Shifting of Reality

Before age 38, I didn't believe that distance healing could be real. After all, it wasn't part of my life experience for 38 years. I thought I knew what was possible or impossible, at least for me. My five senses were my only channels through which I understood and accepted my sense of reality. Things changed when I learned Reiki.

Actually, they didn't change immediately. My first experience of Reiki wasn't that convincing. I didn't know how to feel energy. I wasn't taught how to access my intuition or recognize the way it communicated with me. For a year and a half, I had no confidence in my ability to do Reiki. I also believed that I was just not intuitive at all, and that only people with a special gift of psychic ability could do those things.

Then, I learned the second level of Reiki. In Usui Reiki, the traditional method, level two, the student is taught distance healing

We all get used to experiencing the world a certain, predictable way. That experience forms our expectation of what is "real" and what is not. Much more than what we are told to believe, experience is what holds the power to convince us to open our minds to new paradigms. Paradigms are the beliefs that make up our sense of reality. When we experience something that has, until that point, been outside the contents of that reality, we feel a disturbance. That disturbance encourages us to make a decision.

One choice is to disregard the experience entirely. "Must've been a dream," "That was weird," or "I must have made a mistake in thinking I saw/felt/heard that" are common responses. Then, we go on living as before, expecting things to go back to "normal."

Another choice is to try to induce the experience again, to see if it will reoccur. We might also ask others about the experience, to see if they had anything similar happen to them. We are looking for clues to help validate it. So, we start to experiment . We want to repeat the experience to find out if it is possible that it's real. With an open mind and experimental attitude, we start to tune in more with our intuitive senses. If and when it happens again, we may continue the process until our minds are convinced that the experience is repeatable, consistent, and therefore, we accept it into our version of reality. This is a paradigm shift.

Once we have a paradigm shift, we are faced with more decisions. We may want to connect with others who share our new understanding. We may want to tell friends or family about our new paradigm and see if they are open to sharing it. We may become at odds with those who don't believe that our experience could be real.

Ready? The shift begins here.

HOW DOES REIKI REALLY WORK?

Energy is "guided" by **intention**. Intention is the "driver" for the energy. Intention is the way in which we tell the life force energy how we would like it to work. Our thoughts are powerful, and intention is the **driver** to create change, while **trust in the outcome is the fuel**. That doesn't mean you "have to believe it's going to work" before it will. Rather, trusting that once you set it in motion and intend for a result, something will happen keeps you from blocking the energy. For example, if you intended that Reiki energy should relieve pain, and then in your mind, you are thinking something skeptical, such as, "How is this really going to work? I can't believe that I can really do this," then your own thoughts will block the energy from working. See? Your thoughts are the powerful force here – a natural, and absolutely effective way of creating change. Your thoughts can empower energy to work, or stop it from working.

That's important. Free will is part of this concept. We all have the ability and the power to direct intention the way we want to. Realizing this is a very important shift in thinking for most people who feel that life "just happens" to them.

Intention can be defined as **directive thought**. Intention is what you mean to happen. It's more than a hope or a desire, although it could be defined as thinking toward a desired outcome. Intention can be expressed in many ways, the simplest among them being directive thought. It's "thinking loudly" or "thinking specifically" rather than daydreaming. Another simple way to express intention is through speaking. Giving directions aloud is a way of expressing intention via speaking.

That may sound simple, and it is. Our thoughts and emotions are all made of energy. This energy can affect other people. You've probably had the experience of sensing another person's anger or sadness without that person having told you. Or "catching" another person's happy, bubbly mood after being around that person for a short while. Your energy isn't simply contained in that bubble of an aura of yours. It is also connected to all energy around and in every living thing. All living things and the Earth have life force energy. The Earth has a different vibrational energy, but it has energy too. Hard to believe?

Here's an analogy that could help. Think of life force energy like water. Water is a substance that exists everywhere around us: in the air we breathe, in our bodies, in the sky, seas, as dew on the grass, rain, fog, in fruit and vegetables, and we drink it. It also recycles itself into different forms, and through our bodies, animals, plants, and the ecosystem. The same amount of water exists on the planet now as far back as life existed on the Earth. Let yourself imagine all water molecules connected to each other, regardless of the form of water they embody. Fog, mist, liquid, ice, humidity, clouds, and water content of plants, blood, fluids, and gasses, are all connected to each other. All of these connected water molecules surround and penetrate the Earth and all life as one single interwoven being. Water is the perfect analogy for life force energy.

Life force energy is like water in this analogy. We may not think of it being between us where we don't see it (as humidity in the air), but it is there. Life force energy is also one connected entity. It exists in our bodies as water does—integrated into our cells, organs, breath, and digestive system, and also between, above, below, and around us. When our personal energy becomes off balance, when we have areas in which we are deficient or overactive, life force energy is available to help correct these places and bring us gently into balance. Reiki can restore balance. A Reiki practitioner connects with this unlimited source of life force energy around us all, and intends for it to flow to the areas in need of balancing. That area or areas can be within oneself, or for another person, animal, plant, etc. It also can be sent over any distance or ahead in time, because neither space nor time are limitations when it comes to life force energy.

The way to guide the energy where we would like it to go is via intention. But it is important to know that **intention is only needed for giving the energy a start in the right direction**. After that, it's best to "get out of the way" and let the energy flow where the recipient is ready to receive it. This is similar to giving directions to a cab driver, and then letting that cab driver go to the intended destination. You don't need to push the cab along after giving directions. You can simply observe where the cab is going once you do. That part is called "attention."

When it comes to energy, all you need to do is to set the **intention**, and then place a gentle **attention** on where the energy is being received. An important point is that the practitioner is not as much a "healer" as a "facilitator of healing." The practitioner is offering the Reiki for the recipient to absorb wherever there is a need for balance. The energy does not "zap" out of the practitioner's hands. Reiki flows to the recipient by intention. The practitioner's hands and intuition only serve to inform the practitioner where the Reiki is going as the session is happening. There are no mandatory hand positions, but rather the hands become useful for focusing one's attention on the flow of the Reiki energy**. Wherever the practitioner places his hands, he becomes aware of the ebb and flow of the Reiki in that area.**

The recipient is the actual "healer," because he or she is the one doing the healing. For the practitioner, there's a beautiful dialogue between starting the Reiki flowing and noticing it is being received.

HOW DOES DISTANCE HEALING WORK?

Reiki energy is not limited by physical proximity or time. If that sounds unbelievable to you, think of a cell phone. You can call anyone in the world who has a phone. Its signal carries a frequency immediately across a vast distance. Similarly, you can direct Reiki energy to be received by anyone, anywhere in the world. (Regardless of whether that person has a phone.) The fact that Reiki works over any distance validates the idea that we are all connected by this life force energy that runs through and all around all living things.

Reiki is sent and received by distance via intention. (I bet you knew I would say that). No picture of the person is necessary, and you don't need to already be acquainted with the person to whom you are sending

Reiki. It helps to have the first and last name of the recipient, but even less information can work.

You may wonder how the energy "knows" who to go to once you have directed it. If José in Mexico asks me for a Reiki healing, how will the energy know which José in Mexico should receive it? The answer is that the energy will go to the José who requested it from me, the same José to whom I am intending to send the Reiki.

If I don't know any of the names of the people, but I know something to specify direction with, that can work too. For example, if an ambulance is speeding by and I don't know who is in it, I can ask that Reiki energy be received by the person who needs healing in that ambulance, and his or her medical team, if they are willing to receive it. That's specific enough. Again, it's the intention that gets it there, and you can express that intention in names or descriptions. If you know in any way who you want the energy to go to, the energy will too. So "the person from the grocery store who asked me to send her Reiki today," "the miners trapped in Chile," and "Sally's cousin who is in the hospital" are all valid ways of describing the recipient of the distance Reiki you're offering.

In the energetic world, time is in the eternal present. Although we experience time as linear, because time is actually all one, energy can be in more than one place at the same time. Quantum Physics has verified this as fact. *(Look it up if you want to know more about that. Quantum Physics lessons are beyond the scope of this book.)*

In any case, Reiki energy can very effectively be directed to a person anywhere in the world, now or in the future, by intention.

It can be helpful, when circumstances allow, for you to ask for feedback from the person to whom you're sending distance healing. This is because 1) it's validating for you to know that it's working, and 2) asking for feedback lets the recipient know you care enough to want to know that he or she feels better once you've sent it.

Sometimes it won't be possible to get feedback, however. For example, if you hear on the news that an earthquake has hit Japan, you may want to just send Reiki healing to all the people of Japan who are affected by the earthquake. You won't be expecting anyone from Japan to call and thank you. Or if Aunt Matilda has been rushed to the hospital, you'll want to send her Reiki now, and not worry over whether she felt it or not. In those cases, you just send it, trusting that it will arrive and be received as needed.

WHAT DISTANCE HEALING IS AND ISN'T

Distance healing, also called "absent healing," is a way to channel Reiki or other healing energy to anyone, anywhere in the world. Healing energy is not bound by the laws of time and space, and does not need travel time. It arrives at its destination immediately, directed by the intention of the practitioner.

Distance healing isn't:

- magic. It cannot cure diseases or replace medical treatment or care.

- measurable. Reiki and other energy healing modalities run on a subtle frequency that is not measurable by scientific instruments (yet).

- evil, against religion, or negative in any way. It is a gift by which people can help each other and the world. Anyone who says otherwise doesn't understand this basic principle.

- using the practitioner's own energy. The practitioner is a channel for the energy, directing it by intention to its destination.

- bound by space or time. Distance healing can help a person heal from past events, or gain strength and positive energy for future events. Some use distance healing to heal past life traumas that are affecting them in this lifetime.

Distance healing is:

- gentle in that it cannot cause harm.

- real. It can be experienced by the practitioner and the recipient.

- beneficial. It can help in many ways.

- powerful. It can help people to heal from physical, emotional and spiritual issues.

- available to any energy healer who wishes to channel energy somewhere outside him or herself. The ability is there for those who wish to make use of it.

Distance healing can't:

- change someone's mind

- manipulate someone

- change something that happened. (It can help one to heal from something traumatic, though, or help someone to let go of grudges if that person is ready to let the anger go.)

WHAT ABOUT SYMBOLS?

Let's talk about what symbols are, first. **A symbol is a way of expressing meaning.** Symbols can be in the form of a drawing, an abbreviation, words written or spoken, and even songs like "The Star Spangled Banner" or "Happy Birthday." The purpose of any symbol is to represent meaning.

To explain how words are symbols, think of the word, "cookie." Yum, right? If you did not know that the word "cookie" means that delicious little bite of pastry, it would not mean anything to you. If someone from another country who didn't know that word was asked if he wants a cookie, he would probably look confused…that is, until you held out a cookie, said, "Cookie!" and connected the word to the thing. Now, the word has a meaning. The word, "cookie" **represents** the meaning of the actual thing.

A drawing is also a symbol. Think of a Yield sign, or one with an arrow. Drivers need to know what that symbol means in order to make sense of the message when driving.

Usui Reiki (the traditional method) is usually practiced and taught using symbols to represent meaning, such as "empower the energy here," or "focus on mental/emotional healing now." There are symbols called the Power Symbol, the Mental/Emotional Symbol, and the Distance Healing Symbol. It is taught that drawing, saying, or thinking about these symbols directs the energy to behave in those intended ways. The symbol is used as a "speed-dial" or representation of that meaning. The practitioner puts his trust in the symbol as a way of expressing the intention for a specific result.

The distance symbol used in Usui Reiki is a tool. Symbols themselves don't have intrinsic power. They are **a means for focusing intent** in order to direct the energy. By saying or drawing the distance symbol, you are focusing your intent on distance healing. The same can be done simply by focusing your intent without the symbol.

The distance symbol helps a person to increase his or her confidence level with sending distance energy. Drawing the symbol, the person thinks," I am now going to send energy across a distance to (recipient or intention)." The act of drawing the symbol activates the intent.

Once a person feels confident that he or she can actually intend for the energy to go where he or she wants it, drawing the symbol really isn't necessary. The intent alone is sufficient. The same goes for power symbols, master symbols, and the mental-emotional symbol.

Activating the symbol is the same as expressing intent for the energy to do something specific: strengthen, address mental/emotional concerns, etc. I'm not downplaying the effectiveness of symbols. Their use can be excellent for a Reiki treatment, whether distance or hands-on. I'm simply explaining that symbols are a tool for focusing intention.

Through practice focusing intention, **a practitioner can do this without the symbols** with the same amount of effectiveness. I no longer need to use the distance symbol to channel energy for distance healing. I know it will get there, so I intend and send. It works. Being aware that symbols are a tool can help the practitioner have a conscious understanding of their use. (Also, some Reiki modalities, such as Practical Reiki, do not use any symbols and distance healing is certainly part of Practical Reiki).

With that in mind, one can conclude that the symbols could be exchanged with the intention expressed in words or thoughts, since **the meaning** is what's most important in directing the energy. That meaning, the **intention,** is the reason that it works. Regardless of how the intention is expressed, it is the meaning that makes the energy respond. So, symbols, words, or thoughts will all have the same effect – directing the energy. Practitioners can, therefore, choose how they feel comfortable directing intention, and do that. **It is neither wrong to use, nor to omit, symbols when practicing Reiki.**

Neither you, nor your intended recipient, need to concentrate, meditate, perform elaborate rituals, burn incense, play music, chant, say magic words, or do anything besides intend for the Reiki to be received. While those rituals may make the process a more formal, complex, and some may say "sacred" one, none of those would do a thing without intention. All that's really and truly needed to give and receive an energy healing is intention of the Reiki practitioner to offer Reiki, and the recipient to be willing to receive it. Whether you choose to add one, two, ten, or fifteen ritualized steps into the process really won't change, strengthen, or have any affect at all on the session itself.

The ritual and structure of other methods are really there to help people have a means of directing intention if they don't feel comfortable doing so with words alone. Think of training wheels or speed dial. Each ritual or symbol is a little step in between you and the real thing – the intention. Energy is

ALWAYS directed by intention, so however you decide to direct it – via symbols, words, thoughts, music notes, crystals, color, light, angelic assistance, prayer, or singing Row Row Row Your Boat (kidding – I don't know a method that does that), these are all ways of intending that the energy do this or that. By "do this or that," I mean unblock certain chakras, stream healing to a certain area, strengthen energy, or assist in allowing the recipient to just receive the healing that's needed.

By the way, that's what is really happening here – we are only the faucet, and the energy is the water, and the recipient takes in the water where he is ready for drinking it in. He may need the water to wash away emotional blockages, to soothe away pain, to fill in where a person is parched for receiving energy, or other needs. He may be terribly thirsty but not ready to accept that, and so it's not possible for us to make him drink. He has to be ready to try taking a sip. We are offering the water. The recipient has the ability and choice (conscious or unconscious choice) to receive it where he is ready to do so.

WHAT A PRACTITIONER AND/OR RECIPIENT MIGHT FEEL DURING DISTANCE HEALING

Factors which might temporarily influence an individual's awareness of energy or sensitivity to energetic sensations:

- fatigue
- inexperience (not knowing what to expect to feel)
- over-thinking or over-analyzing each sensation
- health or emotional state which could mask the subtle energy sensations
- being hot or cold, or in pain which could cause the body to just register those physical sensations overwhelming energetic ones (unless the energy is causing the pain to subside, in which case it could be recognized).

- energetic blockages which need to be solved to process energetic sensations
- need for energy – maybe the person has had Reiki recently and doesn't need much at this moment
- denial - people who think that Reiki is fake, and are determined to believe it will have a harder time recognizing it when they do.

It's also important to note that individuals are naturally sensitive to energy in their own way, which could be not at all, or could be involving clairvoyant abilities. In short…everyone's different.

Never be mad at yourself or think you're "doing it wrong" if you don't feel as sensitive to energy as you'd like to be at this moment! Don't compare yourself to others. Just be. If you intend to feel the energy more, you will grow in your energy awareness.

The sensations of energy are subjective and individuals could feel any or a combination of these sensations during energy healing:

- heat
- tingling
- cold
- magnetic-type sensation
- pressure
- warmth

- visible colors moving behind closed eyes
- swirling sensation
- nothing at all

None of these sensations is "wrong," and *even if either person feels nothing at all, it doesn't mean that the energy wasn't received* as much as it reflects on the individual's energetic awareness level at that moment in time.

WHAT ABOUT PERMISSION? IS THAT NEEDED?

Just as you wouldn't want a doctor to force you to take a certain medicine, you wouldn't want to force healing on anyone. Everyone has the free will to refuse or accept a Reiki healing. No matter how tempted you are to just send Reiki to someone who you believe needs it, you shouldn't assume the person wants it. People have their own reasons for wanting or not wanting a certain treatment, whether it is conventional or "alternative" therapy. Some people have religious reasons to refuse energy healing. Others are afraid or not ready to be open to receiving Reiki. The first priority, therefore, is to ask for and receive permission to give or send Reiki energy to whomever you are intending to treat.

At first, this idea may seem silly. It's healing energy! It's good! Everyone should want it! I'm not even touching the person! How could it hurt? But remember: **giving Reiki is doing something.** Because it is real, it matters enough to take it seriously.

In order to get some perspective on this issue, try to put yourself on the other side for a moment. Imagine that you do not know about Reiki. You are at work and are not feeling well. A coworker who you don't know well decides to send some energy to you by distance without letting you know it's coming. Suddenly, you feel strange. There's a heat coursing through you. You feel a little light-headed. You decide you must have a fever and go straight to the doctor because you don't understand these new sensations, instead of going home to rest. If your well-meaning coworker would have taken the time to ask you first, you could have decided whether you wanted to try this healing method. You would have been informed that there could be some new sensations (heat or light-headedness) associated with this energy, so you wouldn't have been alarmed. You might also have been in the right mindset to notice that your original symptoms were relieved, and the ungrounded feeling could be resolved quickly and easily (if only your coworker would have told you how to ground your energy).

Here's another scenario. Your friend's brother, Joe, is having ongoing pain from his recent surgery. You decide to send Joe some Reiki, but don't ask him first. He feels better more quickly than expected, without knowing why. He just assumes that he's a fast healer. Alternatively, you have your friend ask Joe if he would be receptive to you sending some Reiki energy his way to help him with pain relief and healing. Joe is skeptical but agrees. To his surprise, he feels much better. Joe gets in touch with you and you tell him more about Reiki. He tells his doctor about it, decides to continue receiving Reiki, and eventually learns it for himself. He starts offering Reiki to others and talks about how much it has helped him. Because you chose to ask his permission first, there is now another Reiki practitioner in the world sharing healing with others.

And here is a very important example to further illustrate the point about permission. For children (not your own), you need to get permission of the parent or guardian before offering Reiki. **It can be very tempting to ignore this rule!** This is especially true if the child is in your classroom and you are the teacher! Suppose your student comes into class with a headache. Unless you were hired to teach Reiki, you may not offer Reiki just as you may not give the child an over-the-counter pain reliever without parental consent.

Here's a little story that happened to me when I was new to Reiki and excited about being able to help people with this wonderful energy. I was teaching sixth grade in a Sunday School class. One of my students came into class complaining of a headache. I felt sympathy for him and wanted to help. I told him that I might be able to help him feel better. He asked if I had an aspirin, and I said no, but I could offer some energy with my hands by holding them over his head and it might help. The other kids giggled, but he agreed, and I intended Reiki in my thoughts and hovered my hands over his head. I continued to teach my lesson while I had my hands there. After about five minutes, I asked him how he felt. Surprised, he said, "My headache is gone!" I felt triumphant.

I went home and called my Reiki teacher and told her excitedly about helping the student with the headache. To my surprise, she admonished me. "You shouldn't have done that," she said. Taken aback, and a little defensive, I asked her why. She explained that maybe he had a headache because he was coming down with a virus. So I gave him Reiki and his headache went away for now. Suppose he goes home after Sunday School and tells his parents about how his teacher put this energy on his head when he had a headache. Then, that night, he gets sick because he was coming down with a virus anyway and the effects of the short Reiki healing wore off. His parents will think that something weird that the Sunday School teacher did made their kid sick. They'll call the principal the next day and angrily demand to know what kind of strange stuff is going on in that classroom, and who said the teacher could do that to their kid. Boom. I'm in trouble. Needless to say, I didn't sleep well that night. In doing something I thought was nice, I had crossed a line. (Things didn't play out that way, but they could have.)

"Stealth healing" is really not recommended as an ethical practice. Also, for pets that are not your own, you should get permission of the pet's owner before offering Reiki to his or her pet.

Now, there will be times when you just can't get permission. For example, if the intended recipient is in a coma, in surgery, or if you want to send Reiki to the victims of some disaster you heard about on the news. In those cases, err on the side of helping. Send anyway.

There is a "cover your butt" method to get around the permission issue. *This should not be used for your first choice, but only when permission is not possible to obtain.* Here's what you do: When you are setting your intention, ask for Reiki to go to the intended recipient **if his/her Higher Self is willing to receive it**, and if not, that it go to (the Earth, the Universe, etc.). That way, the decision is out of your hands, and you can't mess it up by assuming that someone wants Reiki.

Some practitioners I know say that they ask the intended recipient's Higher Self in their thoughts for permission, and tune in intuitively to sense an answer. I do not recommend this method to you or my students, because I think in many cases, it would be natural to "sense" that of course the person says "yes" because I believe they should. The asker's intuition will be skewed by what the ego wants to do. Some people are intuitive enough to get by with this method, but some are not. I don't trust myself to get a clear answer, due to my own strong desire to help, so I use the method above instead. I also think you can't go wrong with that method because you take your own desires out of the equation.

Some practitioners disagree and say that any Reiki is okay. If the person doesn't want it, it will not get to them. Probably true. Also, you can't request permission to send Reiki to the Earth, or to a country with many victims of some kind of disaster. It is my thinking that in the case of the Earth, or disaster healing, send as much as you can. While I see the point of the Reiki practitioners who would send any and all Reiki to anyone and anything because healing is good, I still just believe that permission is a good thing. Would I want to be the recipient of random Reiki sent to me without my knowledge or permission? Not always. Maybe it depends. Knowing that I feel that way is what puts me on the side of those who support permission.

THE BASIC "FORMULA" FOR SENDING DISTANCE REIKI:

"Intend and Send" This is the basic formula for distance healing. **To intend**: say to your higher self (in your thoughts, specifically, as though you are saying it out loud), "I am sending distance Reiki to (name)." You may change or add details as you desire, such as "I am sending distance Reiki to Jon for healing and relief from pain." Or, "I am sending distance Reiki to the universe to open channels for more work opportunities to come to me." Whatever you want the Reiki to go to, just intend it.

Also, a practitioner may intend to observe the energy of the recipient during the sending, and use scanning to see that the need has resolved after the treatment.

SCANNING

Scanning (called Byosen Scanning in Usui Reiki), is a very good way to get a feel for a person's energy. It can tell the practitioner in what place(s) a person needs more Reiki, and give information about a person's state of being. This can be done with a surrogate or by just imagining the shape of a person's body. First, start sending Reiki to your intended recipient, following the "intend" directions above. Then, intend "scanning."

Slowly move your hand down the front of the person's body from the top of the head all the way down past the feet. Take mental note of any places in which the sensation in your hand changes as you do so. You might feel tingles as your hand moves over some parts of the body, or heat, cold, or other sensations. Some people are more visual in their energy sensitivity and those people may receive visual cues about the energy, such as colors or other visual sensations. All are valid. All represent a place the person is in need of healing. (In person, scan the space directly above the recipient's body, 3 inches or so above without touching.)

I usually will remain at each location where I notice a difference in the energy, and send Reiki there until the tingles of the energy flow subside. Then I move to the next place. I have noticed that if I experience lots of tingling around the person's head, that the recipient may have a headache or lots of head congestion. If I feel lots of tingling over a person's chest or stomach, there could be either a lot of anxiety or some digestive distress. In any case, they're all good reasons to direct Reiki to these places. Stay in this area until you feel a change. That will indicate that the appropriate amount of healing energy has been received.

Believe in yourself and your ability to do this. Your sensitivity will increase with practice. If you don't feel anything, that's ok too, because either the person has no outstanding areas of need, or you should just do a general treatment for that person.

Although a Reiki treatment without scanning a person's energy could be complete in itself, the practitioner who wishes to receive energetic information about the needs of the recipient may wish to combine Reiki with scanning during treatment, in order to focus treatment on a specific area. It's perfectly ok to combine or experiment with the Reiki energies in any modality, as Reiki plays well with other healing methods, and will only serve to enhance the healing potential. Reiki will never reduce effects of a treatment, or cause harm in any way.

THREE WAYS TO SEND DISTANCE REIKI RELATIVE TO TIME:

1. In Real Time. This means that I am sending Reiki healing to another person (or people), to be received now, at this moment. This can be referred to as "intend and send." First, you turn on the Reiki by thinking or saying "Reiki on." Then, you intend "Distance healing for (name)" and add any Situation/Qualities intention if there is one. Then you simply sit a few minutes with the energy flowing until you feel it is done. Usually, this will happen in 5-7 minutes.

For example: I receive a call from my husband, who is at work and has a headache. He asks if I will send him Reiki to help relieve his headache. I intend "Reiki on. Healing for Evan Langholt, to relieve the pain of his headache," and then I sit quietly for a few minutes, feeling the Reiki flow to

Evan. I hold my hands with my palms facing each other, because when I do this, I am placing my attention on my palms and the energy sensations I feel there. I know from the sensations in my palms that the Reiki is flowing to Evan, and also when it stops. The energy is starting and going to Evan right now, as I intend it to.

The "Real Time" method is good for any time you are wanting to send Reiki now to be received now. It doesn't matter whether the recipient is paying attention or not, the Reiki is going to that person immediately when you are sending it.

2. Preset. This method is for when you want the Reiki energy to begin working at a predetermined date and time in the future, but you want to send it now. To do this, first, turn on the Reiki by intending "Reiki on." Then, intend "Distance Reiki for (name) to be received at (date, time)." If the person is in another time zone, you can add "in his/her time zone" to the instructions. Of course, if you have a situational intention to add, that can be added as well. See the examples below.

Example #1: my daughter, Rayna, has a math test that she's worried about (even though she studied), on Thursday at 1:00 pm. She asks me to send her Reiki on Thursday at 1:00. But I will be teaching at that time, so I can't send it to her in real time. I choose to preset the Reiki for her by sending it now, intended for her to receive it on Thursday at 1:00 pm. I intend, "Reiki on. Distance Reiki for Rayna, to be received on Thursday at 1:00 pm, for mental clarity and confidence." Then I sit quietly for a few minutes with my palms facing each other, feeling the energy flow. On Thursday, the Reiki will begin flowing for Rayna automatically at 1:00 pm as scheduled, without Rayna or me needing to do anything more. Think of the Preset Reiki method as setting a lamp on a timer device, so that it will turn on at a specific time automatically.

Example #2: You can also use the preset method for yourself. If I know that I have an important meeting on Monday morning at 9:00 am, I will preset Reiki to be received by me on Monday morning at 9:00 am. Or I might even start it flowing at 8:45 am so I don't walk into the meeting nervous! That way I don't have to remember to give myself Reiki at that time while I'm trying to remember whatever I'm supposed to talk about. It'll just be there for me, starting automatically, even if I forget that I had sent it to myself.

3. Queued. This method allows you to send Reiki ahead of time, and the energy will be received *when the recipient intends to receive it*. This needs to happen intentionally. I jokingly call it "DVR Reiki" because it's just like recording a healing ahead of time, and then when the person it was recorded for is ready, he presses the "play" button by intending for the Reiki to begin. The energy stays in the recipient's energy field until it is "called in" by the recipient intending "I am now receiving the Reiki sent by (your name)."

Truthfully, the recipient could simply say, "Reiki, GO!" or "I want my Reiki NOW!" and the Reiki would start at that moment. Why? Because they are all ways to express the **intention** to receive the Reiki healing, and intention is what matters! But, I like to make it a little more formal by telling the recipient to use a full sentence to intend to receive the energy. Also, it seems a little flip to have the person say "Reiki GO!" so he may not take it seriously and it could make him doubtful that it would work if he did.

Here's how queuing a Reiki healing is done: First, intend "Reiki on." Then, intend "Reiki healing for (name), queued for (him/her) to receive when (he/she) is ready." Then simply hold your palms facing each other and feel the energy flowing until it stops. Your part is done!

You'll want to give your recipient some directions

for how to receive the Reiki. I usually give these instructions to the recipient: *"When you are ready to receive the energy, please rest in a quiet place, and intend once softly, 'I will now receive the healing sent by Alice.' The energy will begin immediately upon your intention to receive. Just gently tune in and receive the healing energy. The best way to describe the mindset is be an observer and just notice what's different for the next half hour or so. The session will last around 25 minutes. I recommend that you rest in a quiet place, undisturbed by phone or TV. Soft music is fine if you prefer it. There is no need to repeat the statement, meditate, concentrate, or otherwise. Just place a gentle awareness on your physical and emotional state to feel the energy working. It helps to close your eyes, because some people experience color changes or images with their eyes closed during a Reiki healing. If you fall asleep, you will still receive the healing, but won't be as aware of the experience (which is the fun part, I think)."*

I also give the recipient some information about how Reiki may feel: *"Reiki energy is a subjective experience. It may feel: warm, tingly, like waves of soothing feelings, make you feel "lighter" emotionally, relaxing, release pain, relieve stress, increase clarity, you may see colors, and/or have a strong sense of well being come over you. You may sense presences around you or have other sensations. It depends on the ways in which you are sensitive to energy."*

I love queuing a healing because I know that the

recipient will be paying attention to how she feels during the session, and will be able to give me some feedback afterward about how the energy was experienced. Feedback can be very useful.

Ending a Sending

When you are through with the distance healing session, close it however you would close an in-person healing session. This may mean drawing a power symbol in the air, sending healing to the entire aura, and then putting your hands together in "Gassho" position, or simply putting your hands down and intending the sending to be finished. Do what feels right to you. There isn't a wrong answer, but it is good to do something to indicate that you are finished with the sending. Even a little "thank you" to the energy, Spirit, guides, or your higher self for the ability to send this healing energy treatment, is a nice gracious way to end a sending.

WAYS TO STRENGTHEN DISTANCE HEALING PRACTICE

- **Ignore naysayers.** Their issues with understanding or accepting the reality of Reiki are not yours. Be confident in your own understanding. Reiki doesn't require belief. It is. Others have to find their own path, and their negative energy doesn't have to be yours or a reflection on you.

- **Have an open mind:** The limitations of Reiki have yet to be discovered. The more you trust the energy is there, and you are a channel for the energy, the more you'll learn to recognize the sometimes subtle sensations of the energy flowing. If your previous understanding of reality did not include higher beings, Reiki guides, angels, past lives, clairvoyance, or the power of crystals, work on opening your mind to the possibility of these aspects of a higher reality. It's okay not to know. You may miss things if you deny the reality of what you don't know.

- **Practice:** Channel energy every day. Reiki your food and drinks before eating. Reiki your plants, pets, house, doorways. Send Reiki to intentions for positive energy for future events, to open doorways to new opportunities, and anything to which you aspire. Join the Distance Healing Network (www.the-dhn.org) and volunteer to send Reiki during the week to a person who has requested it. The more you use it, the more you'll feel it. This is very true with Reiki (as with other things a person wishes to learn).

- **Meditation:** There are some great Reiki meditations, but go ahead and just find quiet time to sit and relax. Call in the energy and place your hands together (called "Gassho" position). Tune in to your breath, and slow down. Feel your physical sensations throughout your body, and be aware of your thoughts and feelings. Then let them go and just be in the moment as the energy flows. Try visualizing the flow of energy to your third eye chakra (center of the forehead), which is the center of energy intuition. Ask questions of your higher self, and listen for answers. Accept what you hear, even if you think it's your own imagination answering you.

If you want to grow in your energetic awareness, just continue to practice connecting with the energy. Here are some suggestions for doing this:

SEVEN TECHNIQUES FOR DISTANCE HEALING:

Reminder: energy is directed by intention. The way one chooses to focus on making their intention clear is only a choice. Think of it like drinking water from a glass. You could choose to use a blue twisty straw, a plain white straw, a hat that holds the drink on top and has a long straw coming down, or a straw with the bendy neck. Either will get the drink to your mouth. It's just a different way for the drink to get there. Same with channeling energy. You are the channel. The means are your choice.

Here are some different ways in which energy healers focus their intent on distance healing. None is wrong or superior to another. All are valid, because they are the chosen technique of the person using them. Try different ones to find what works best for you.

1. The surrogate method

Have a doll, teddy bear, or pillow. Lay it on your knees. This will represent the person (in a smaller version) that you are treating. Call in the Reiki, intend to channel distance healing to (name) for (ailment or greatest good). Intend that the surrogate you've chosen represent that person's comparable parts. Treat the surrogate with a hands-on treatment, intending the energy to reach the intended recipient. You may scan, and turn the surrogate over when you need to. When finished, do whatever technique you choose to intend to close the healing. (Some draw the power symbol, some intend the healing be done and the Reiki "turn off").

Try some different ways and see which you like the best as your method. It's okay to switch methods, try different ways, modify any of these, or come up with your own.

2. The invisible person method

Call in the energy, intend to channel distance healing to (name), for (ailment or greatest good). Visualize the shape of a person's body in front of you. The shape can be upright or laying down, whichever is easier. Intend that the body shape you are visualizing represent that person's comparable parts. Scan the body shape, intending to scan the person. You may intend to scan each part in turn, using intention to name that part as you go. For example, intending "scanning head" as you scan the visualized head area, etc.

3. The tiny recipient inside the hands method

Call in the energy, draw or intend the distance symbol (if using), and intend to channel distance healing to (name). For this method, you may intend the energy reach a group of people, if you are sending to a list or a number of people at once.

No scanning is used in this method.

Intend the energy to be channeled to the recipient(s) in as much as they need it, for their greatest good and healing. Feel the energy flow between your hands, holding them this way as long as the energy flows, or until you feel the treatment is done.

4. The knee or thumb surrogate method

Do as the surrogate method (#1 above), but instead of a doll, pillow or teddy bear, use your own knee (or thumb) as a surrogate to represent the intended recipient. When using your knee, the kneecap is the head, and the rest of the body follows down about to the middle of the thigh. When using your thumb to represent the recipient, the top of the thumb is the head and the rest is the body. This is ideal for sending Reiki when in a public place. It's a bit more challenging to use scanning with the thumb surrogate method though!

Do closing in your chosen way.

5. The name on paper method

Write the recipient's name on a piece of paper, intending the energy to go to that person. Then hold the paper or beam Reiki to the paper with the person's name on it. This is simple to do, and if the person has a specific request like "relieve stomach pain" you can also write this on the paper.

6. The intend and send method

In Practical Reiki, one simply intends that the energy go to so-and-so, adds anything to the intention if there is more specifics (like John's headache), and holds his hands palms facing together while the energy flows, knowing it is going to that intention. One may speak the intention aloud, if desired. Personally, I just think my intention and let it flow. Works every time.

7. The intentionless meditation method

For this method, one should be very comfortable with meditation. First step is to get into meditation, however works best for you. Just take a few minutes, 5-10, perhaps, to get to the deep, quiet, and present undistracted state.

Next, intend to connect with the recipient. Intend only to be connected with that person in the "all that is" ONENESS of all. Be in this mental and energetic space with that person, wanting only the highest and best for that person, whatever it may be.

Observe what you experience in this place of total connection with the Universal Oneness energy. When you feel a sense of closure, you are done.

VOLUNTEER ORGANIZATIONS LOOKING FOR DISTANCE HEALERS

1. The Distance Healing Network (http://www.the-dhn.org)

I am a proud Group Leader of the DHN. I have a group of energy healers who are in my charge. I am sent a list of cases each week, which I divide and assign one to each member of my group. The cases are requests from a people somewhere in the world who have requested energy healing for a specific need. My group members send Reiki to their assigned person throughout the week. The DHN answers thousands of requests each year. To join a group, you have to apply and when there is an opening, they will contact you.

2. The Reiki Page (http://reiki.7gen.com/)

This is a yahoo group: Remote Healing Requests, which is open to any energy healer who wishes to receive requests for healing. I receive them in daily digest format, and there is no obligation to respond to any or all of the requests. It's a good place to start if one wants to have someone to send distance Reiki to, although you won't be receiving feedback

3. **We are One World Monthly World Healing (http://therapeuticreiki.com/blog/)** This is a group of energy healers around the world who band together once a month at the appointed time (time-zone coordinated) and send healing to the world together from their locations for one hour. Many leave feedback afterward, and it is known to be a powerful experience. Good practice for a good cause. It's kinda cool too to know that you're part of a group of people doing the same thing at that moment in time for the good of the world.

OTHER USES FOR DISTANCE HEALING

As I mentioned before, there are no limits to the ways in which you can incorporate distance healing into your life. Whether it's for a person, issue, or request, it can only be beneficial to find opportunities every day for practice with the energy.

Here are a few possible uses, but there are many more.

- to help clear the room, house, office, car, or where you are going of negative energy
- to a future doctor or dentist appointment to reduce your anxiety or pain
- to make a cheap bottle of wine taste better (try it!!)
- to purify water with positive

energy (this also makes tap water taste better)
- to help a fussy baby get to sleep
- to help a child who can't sleep get to sleep (can you tell I'm a mom?)
- to soothe a child after being upset (distance works for this)
- when you can't do hands-on (like while driving)
- to help release grudges or anger
- to help sever unhealthy ties to past events or toxic people
- to help get over a phobia
- to help release emotional baggage
- to help plants grow more healthy
- to help pets or hurt animals
- to soothe hot flashes from menopause
- to restore energetic balance
- to shed negative energy from the day
- to boost confidence for an upcoming job interview or meeting
- to help manifest a goal

EXCELLENT REIKI RELATED WEBSITES:

http://www.aetw.org/ **James Deacon's Reiki web resource**. This is the most informative website I've ever come across. It has information about every type of Reiki, the history of Reiki, how to do many types of meditation, Reiki symbols, and many, many articles about Reiki. It is completely text-based, but I can't recommend anything more than this website.

http://reikiawakeningacademy.com **Reiki Awakening Academy -** This is the online school that I founded. We teach live online, and offer recorded classes in many
intuitive, healing, metaphysical, and professional subjects. Many of our classes offer CEUs and we also have several Certificate Programs.

http://www.reiki.org/ **The International Center for Reiki Training** is a website run by William Rand, one of the most recognized Reiki authorities out there. His website features strong support for Reiki practitioners and teachers, as well as scientific articles on the reality of Reiki, a magazine, Reiki training manuals, and much more. A person could spend months there and not read it all. My Usui Reiki training came from this lineage.

http://reikiawakening.com **Reiki Awakening -** this is my Reiki website and it's the place where I offer distance healing, additional attunements, Intuitive Counseling Sessions, Angel Card Readings, resources, and more. Come on over!

RECOMMENDED RESOURCES

REIKI FALSE BELIEFS EXPOSED FOR ALL: Misinformation Kept Secret by a Few Revealed by Steve Murray This is an excellent book on Reiki that helps people develop a strong and healthy understanding of the various beliefs about Reiki and what is and isn't true.

Practical Reiki: for balance, well-being and vibrant health by Alice Langholt. This is the manual for the method I developed from Kundalini Reiki. It includes information on all three levels, as well as chapters on understanding your intuition, and chakras. This book also won second place for "Best Reiki Book" in the 2012 About.com Reader's Choice Awards.

Reiki: The True Story, an Exploration of Usui Reiki by Don Beckett. This book clears up so many misconceptions about who Mikao Usui, the founder of Reiki healing was, and how he taught. I found it refreshing, informative, and learned a lot! I had the fortune to have a wonderful conversation with Don Beckett, and he also wrote a testimonial for my *The Practical Reiki Companion* workbook.

Manifesting Made Simple

How to Engage the Universe in Bringing Your Best Life into Being

Alice Langholt
Reiki Master Teacher
Author of the Award-winning book
Practical Reiki: for balance, well-being, and vibrant health

DEDICATION

I dedicate this book to my husband, Evan, for being open-minded enough to try this and prove that it works.

The Lightworker's Compendium V.1

CONTENTS

Introduction	66
What is Manifesting?	71
Desire	76
Intention	82
Expectation	92
Action	94
The Super-Fast Way	97
Resource Charts for Intention Wording	101

INTRODUCTION

When I learned Reiki energy healing, my mind was opened. Reiki was the gateway to expanding my view of life. I began to realize that people are more powerful than I'd previously believed. And, there were so many more tools to healing, wellness, and a better life than I had ever known. It felt like discovering a trunk of magic tools, and all I had to do was learn to use them.

As a skeptical person, for every new holistic or metaphysical technique I learned, I needed to try it over and over again until I had enough data with positive, consistent results to develop confidence that it worked. Then, I needed to teach it to someone else, to find out if it would work for that person too. If it did, I knew that it could be taught, shared, and trusted.

When *The Secret* came out, and "Law of Attraction" was the buzzword going around the New Age discussion boards, it attracted my attention. Our family was living in Ohio, constantly struggling to support our family, and stressed. I read about vision boards, writing a check to yourself from the Universe, visualization, affirmations, and more.

I began to study what was out there, and started looking for the common ingredients in all of these manifesting methods. I searched for the point behind the rituals, practices, and tools that were being used. I decided to experiment with the simplest ways possible to apply the concepts that the practices were meant to produce.

One reason that I was looking for the simplest way to make these things work is that I'm a very busy person. Another reason is that I am not crafty. I don't like to cut out pictures and glue them onto paper. I wanted to use these concepts as quickly and simply as possible to achieve the results they were intended for. The best way to do this was by understanding the reasons behind each of the practices common to the methods that had been reported to produce effective results. So, I looked for the reasons, the concepts, and chose simple ways to apply the concepts to a practice that could be done quickly, with measurable results.

What resulted from my study of the methods, extracting the common ingredients, and testing them is this practical approach to manifesting, which I call Manifesting Made Simple.

The most convincing test result – my husband's job offer

As I mentioned earlier, when we lived in Ohio, we were in a place of financial and career-related frustration. My husband, Evan, was overqualified for the job he was doing, and there didn't seem to be any other jobs open which were more appropriate for his level of education and experience.

He was complaining about this one evening, when I said to him, "Instead of complaining, why don't you manifest what you want?" He replied that he didn't know how, so I gave him my notes and told him to read them, then try it out if he wanted. A little while later, he told me he was going to try it.

Evan worked on the techniques, which you'll read about in the coming chapters. Two weeks later, he received a message via LinkedIn. It was from an organization in Washington, DC where he had interviewed for an Executive Director position four years before. The message said that the person they had hired didn't work out, and they wondered if Evan was available and might be interested in applying again. This was – exactly – the position he had wanted. He did interview, and was selected for the job. We moved to the Washington, DC area four months later. It was the very best move for our whole family, at the very best time. (Had he gotten the job four years earlier, it would have been awful because Evan's mom became ill with cancer, and we needed to be in Ohio to care for her through the process of her treatment, and her passing, and dealing with all that was involved emotionally, logistically, etc. at that time.)

The ways in which all of the details regarding the move and settling into our new home fell into place were beyond logic. It was clear throughout the process that we were being supported by what some would call "good fortune," or "incredible luck." I saw it as things aligning as we had manifested. The number of seeming "coincidences" were too staggering to be credited to chance. Something bigger was happening.

Over the next few years, I used the techniques in this book to help my businesses thrive, as well as help things work out for many other goals, such as family trips, my son's Bar Mitzvah party, and new opportunities.

Most recently, I further condensed the techniques into a 3-minute method that I can do in the car, the shower, or whenever I have some brief alone time. That, too, is included in this book.

I hope that you will try this for yourself and notice the shifts in your own life. Understanding how things work is key to using them effectively. Like energy healing, and using your own intuition, manifesting is a skill that we are all capable of using. We have a relationship with the Universe of which we are a part. Learn it and try it. Notice the shifts. Repeat until you see that the results surpass "random chance." Let your own experience convince you that it works.

And, of course, have fun and enjoy the process!

WHAT IS MANIFESTING?

It's always important to define what is being discussed. So, let's check the dictionary definition of "manifest," the verb. Going to Google for a quick definition check, the top result shows up embedded at the top of the first page of results.

First, it says, "[*with object*] display or show (a quality or feeling) by one's acts or appearance; demonstrate: *Ray manifested signs of severe depression.*"

Here, the word refers to something that appears, shows up, or is evident visually or from behavior.

The definition continues, "[*no object*] (of an ailment) become apparent through the appearance of symptoms: *a disorder that usually manifests in middle age."*

Here, we see that symptoms or circumstances can point to evidence of the existence of something.

Finally, the definition concludes, "[*no object*] (of a ghost or spirit) **appear:** *one deity manifested in the form of a bird."*

From this last part, the definition refers to something appearing into being where it had not existed before.

To summarize, manifesting is to cause something to appear or occur. That is going to be our working definition.

Why would we want to manifest something? In order to make it happen. There's something that we want, which we do not as of yet have, and that is the thing which we want to bring into our life. This "bringing it into our life" is the process we will be learning to do in this book.

What might we want to manifest? It could be a goal, or it could be material, like money, or could be a job doing a specific kind of work. Other examples could be a bigger house, a newer car, or new opportunities. Manifestation is one way of doing something about it on an energetic level to help bring it about and that's really what we're talking about here.

What is the process of manifesting about? It is about **creating the energy needed to bring into one's life the object of one's desires or goals.** Everything is energy. Matter is energy. Thoughts and emotions are energy too. All energy is interconnected and affects itself. It vibrates. There are an infinite number of possibilities for every moment until that possibility aligns, comes into being, and leads to the next possibility. When potential outcomes are in resonance with the same vibration as the energy around them, then that most likely outcome will be the one that appears.

Creating the energy then means affecting the flow of the creation energy of the universe by **creating a harmonic resonance with that goal in order to align events to bring about this goal.** In this book, you'll learn ways to intentionally create a harmonic resonance which will result in the energy creating events that are most likely to bring your goal into being. Being in harmony energetically with the things that we want, engages the Universe to easily make those things appear. Affecting the energy of the Universe to vibrate with the same frequency our goal will help to create the right energy to bring it into play.

Four essential ingredients are involved in the process of manifesting. By intentionally focusing on each one, desired changes can result. You'll see these changes materializing in many ways. Among the things you can expect are:

- seeming coincidences – events lining up in surprising ways
- signs – noticing things that seem suddenly significant in relation to your thoughts, questions, or goals. These things could be song lyrics, bumper stickers, objects in odd places, an article providing information which comes across your screen or inbox, basically anything that catches your attention that seems related could be named as a sign
- opportunities to take action to move your goal forward to the next step – this could be a call, an email, or a course or conference related to your goal, or it could be an interview opportunity, or networking meeting, or a job opportunity that you could apply for. In short, this is a time to take action to move things further toward realizing your goal.

The four essential ingredients, which will be explained fully in the coming chapters, are **Desire, Intention, Expectation, and Action.** When all of these are aligned toward your goal, manifesting will be the result.

Why does this work? Manifesting works because we are all part of the creative force of the Universe. What does that mean? Basically, we are all part of this one creative energy that comprises life. Our free will is our creative power. What we can imagine, we can bring to life because we are all equally capable of creating. By using this process, we are engaging in the natural process of creation, and as creative beings, we have the power to do so.

DESIRE

There's something you want. Maybe it's a better job, or the money for a vacation, or to find a person to be in a relationship with, or you want a problem in your life to be solved. Maybe you're looking for more opportunities to do the work you love, or more time to spend doing the activities you enjoy. The first part of this process is defining what you want.

Defining what you want is more than saying something like, "I want a better job," or "I want more money." There are a few important ways to do this which affect the process.

You want a better job. What are the characteristics that would make this a better job? What would make a job great for you? This is a question about qualities rather than specifics. For instance, rather than saying, "I want a job at XYZ Company," it is better to say,

"I'm ready for a job where I can use my skills to help others, be respected, be creative, and receive compensation and appreciation for my work." Those are the **qualities** of the goal – *how it would feel* to be working in the job that would be great for you. Thinking in terms of the qualities of the goal invites the universe to bring you the best possible outcome.

This is an emotionally-connected process, rather than a purely intellectual one. In fact, creative energy always involves some measure of emotional content. Think of any creative activity. Making music, dancing, drawing, singing, writing poetry, and even cooking involve putting something of yourself into expressing an experience. The process must have a component of emotional energy, or else it will fall flat. It will be "dry," or "dull."

Defining your desire is already a creative process when you are thinking in terms of the **qualities** of your desired outcome. You would feel fulfilled, you would feel happy with these qualities in place. As you define the qualities, imagine what it would really be like, and let yourself actually experience these emotions as you imagine it. This is an energetic creative activity, and needs to be, in order for it to be effective. We are looking to affect the energy of creation, and creativity is emotional.

It's best to do this when you have time, and can be relaxed. Have you ever tried to be creative when you're stressed? It's hard! Instead, the creative flow is effortless when we are relaxed and can be in a playful state of mind. Sit quietly for a moment. Breathe, and give yourself permission to use your imagination without judgment. Judging the process while in it is blocking. Just like brainstorming is done without analyzing, in a playful mindset, this activity is best done when you can just relax and imagine having what you want in detail. A meditational state is where creation energy has the strongest, most unrestricted flow. That's where you want to be for this exercise.

If meditation is difficult for you, that's fine. Just be relaxed and don't multitask. Focus exclusively on this process. It doesn't take a long time. If you get distracted in the middle, just bring your attention back.

You might think, "But, wanting something is an emotion." Yes, that is true. However, wanting is an emotion of lack. You don't want to present this energy to the Universe. The Universe reflects back the energy that we show it. Whatever we focus on grows stronger. Another way I've heard it said is that the Universe says, "Yes" to whatever we mean. In all of these ways of thinking, focusing on lack will bring in more lack. So, stop thinking words like want or need. Stop feeling crappy because you don't have what you are desiring. Don't focus on *want*. Focus on **how it would feel to have it.**

I'm not asking you to lie to yourself and say that you have something when your mind is thinking, "No, I don't have it! This is a lie!" I'm asking you to **imagine what it would be like to have it**. Using your imagination to enjoy the idea of things being as you want them is a creative and positive exercise. You aren't declaring that you have it already. You are imagining what life would be like if you did have it.

One of the ways people get tripped up when trying things like affirmations is that the mind recognizes a false statement and doesn't accept it. So, make sure that you understand that you are engaging in an imaginative exercise, rather than lying to yourself. We'll talk about effective use of affirmations in the next chapter.

Since we are part of the energy of other people as well as the Universe, it's easier to manifest something that is harmonic with the highest and best of others as well as yourself. So, with that in mind, when you are defining what it is you desire, ask yourself if it is in your best to have it, and if it is also for the best of others.

For instance, if having a new job in Arizona would cause your family to have to move 500 miles away, and the hardship of that is in the way of this being in the best interest of all of you, that might be harder to manifest. Or , if winning the lottery would cause so much undue publicity and stress that it would not really help you out in the long run (as is the case for many who actually do win the lottery), you might be better off manifesting financial abundance from the work you love to do instead.

If what you want is for the best of you and all who would be concerned in the process of having what you desire, this process is going to carry stronger creative energy. Remember that creative energy is the fuel for bringing things into being.

Here's one example: deciding that you desire a job where you're using your skills and talents to help people have better lives, and help support an organization in achieving its goals. In this example, you are fulfilled doing the work that you enjoy, and helping others makes this in the best interest of more than just yourself.

Get clear on as many aesthetics of your desire as you can. What would it look like, sound like, feel like, to have this? What would your day be like? What details do you care about including that would make you feel fantastic about having this desire fulfilled?

As you imagine these details, really let yourself be in that mind space. Feel the feelings of the version of yourself who is actually there. Give your creative mind permission to fully immerse in the experience of imagining this, enough so that you actually feel happy, fulfilled, and grateful to be there. Remember, you aren't lying to yourself; you are creating. That begins in the imagination, and it's fueled by positive emotions.

Do you need to write this down, or draw it in any way? You don't have to, but you can if you want to. Some people find it useful to write a narrative, list, or draw a picture of their desire fulfilled. Whatever helps you anchor what you imagine in your mind is fine. The choice is yours, and there's no wrong way unless it feels wrong to you. If it's easier to recall what you desire by doing any of those things, go ahead. **The most important part of this process is what happens in your mind and emotions.**

INTENTION

I would say that this is the most important ingredient of them all. Intention is how you will express the desire to the Universe. You already started the process in the last step. In this step, you will expand on it.

This step is a logical extension of the last part when you were imagining yourself in the position of having your goal achieved. The idea is to use your mind to help you tell the Universe about your desire. Think of it as placing your order. You want your order to be specific. The Universe communicates in an emotional language, so you need to speak in that language to the Universe. Remember that emotions are energy. Words are only energetic when they carry some kind of emotional weight. That emotional weight is the meaning behind the words, whether it be joy, anger, fear, disgust, or sadness, words carry power when there is emotion of some kind infused in them. First have the details in place, then fuel the details with emotional energy. That is how to make and send your order using the Universe's "system."

In this step, you will more fully describe to the Universe what it is you are intending to bring into your life. There are many ways to do this. Before we get into the various methods of expressing your message, though, it's important to mention the importance of word choice and the message the words convey through their emotional content.

It's important to be aware of how you are communicating your idea as you are sending your message to the Universe. If, during your imagining, you notice your mind thinking something limiting, such as, 'This will never work," or "What if this doesn't work? I'll feel like such an idiot," then bring yourself back to the task of allowing, even just for now, the possibility that it can happen. The reason for this is that worrying is an emotional energy that blocks the process. Worrying is imagining something negative, with emotion. That's some powerful manifesting energy, but not the kind that you want to activate. So, it's important to let that go right away.

Don't beat yourself up if you realize you are worrying, but take a moment to recognize that you are worrying, and then **tell yourself that you're just going to give this a try and see if it works**. Doing this tends to help you put worries aside fairly easily.

There are other self-limiting beliefs that can muddy up the message you're sending out. If you don't feel worthy of having what you desire, that will block you from having it. The Universe isn't going to send you something that you are telling the Universe that you don't want or deserve. It's like saying please, and then saying, "Never mind, no thank you, I really shouldn't." If you find yourself worrying, or don't really believe it's possible that you actually could, should, or will have what you desire, then it would be best to do some work on clearing those ideas before you begin the manifesting process.

Doubts, worries, and self-limiting beliefs stem from fear. The fear might be fear of disappointment. For instance, you might be thinking, "If this doesn't work, I'll be disappointed, and feel like such a failure all over again!" Or, the fear might be of overwhelm, as in, "If I really get this assignment, it might be too much for me and I'll fail." The fear might also be of success, believe it or not! You might be thinking, "If I get this, my friends will be jealous, or I won't have time for my family, or I might be expected to perform at this level all the time."

How can you clear doubts, worries, and self-limiting beliefs? Many techniques could help you, but the easiest one is to recognize that you're feeling any of those things, and then thank that belief for trying to protect you from disappointment or overwhelm, and let it go. Make a positive, reassuring statement in its place. If you need more intensive work on clearing, you could try Reiki healing, EFT (Emotional Freedom Technique, also known as "tapping"), or some meditation with affirmations, or you can work with an Intuitive Counselor, or get some therapy, whichever method you feel comfortable using to help you.

Words hold energy, as I mentioned before. That energy is going to be important in the ways you express your intention in this step. With that in mind, it's best to avoid words that express lack. If you are telling the Universe, "I want more money," you are expressing the message of **wanting** most of all. Remember, whatever we say to the Universe, the Universe says, "yes" to. So if we say, "I want" the Universe will respond by amplifying wanting – or lack. Oops. Not want you meant, right?

Here's a list of words to avoid when you are describing your desire to the Universe:

- want
- need – this is even worse than "want" because it has a desperate kind of energy to it
- hope – this is a word that has a real frequency of doubt going through it.
- wish – this is a word that basically means that you don't really believe it will happen in real life
- pray – like a combination of wishing and begging. Don't get me wrong – prayer is good in the right context. In manifesting, though, we are going to focus on already having that prayer answered, so it's not about asking.
- please – again, we aren't really asking. We're placing a specific order. Please is a word that is associated with asking. While politeness is lovely, in this process of visualization, "thank you" is more appropriate than "please".

As a reminder, the following emotions must be avoided in this step:
- fear
- doubt
- desperation
- worry

- "what if"s – as in "But, what if it doesn't work?" or "What will I do if this happens, but that doesn't?"
- begging

To stay positive, you can use Affirmations. Affirmations are great when you can believe them. Affirmations are little statements that state what you want in the present tense, as if it's already true. The problem that some people face with affirmations is that they don't believe them when they say them. Their inner snarky voice replies, "yeah, right" after they say their affirmation, and they try to ignore it, but it's there. For instance, if a person is feeling low on money, and tries saying an affirmation, "I am wealthy," there's not much chance that person is going to really believe it at all. So, the snarky voice will call that out, and the affirmation carries no positive emotional weight to it at all – on the contrary, it actually sets them back because their feeling about it has reinforced their belief that it's false.

A better way to use affirmations is to affirm something that you can accept mentally as well as emotionally. If you're feeling low on money, you can say, "I'm ready to accept more money into my life now." I bet you could easily agree on that one. Or you can affirm, "I'm working on ways to attract the

money to cover all of my needs and more."
Affirmations are good for increasing confidence, and dispelling self-limiting thoughts that can block your manifesting power. They also increase positivity, and that is the kind of emotional fuel you want working for you.

For the imagining process of the Desire and Intention steps, think of Method Acting. In Method Acting, you're playing a role. To play the role well, you get into character by replicating the emotions within yourself that you'd feel in this character's situation. You work on creating actual, true emotions, to express through the character's actions and dialog, which will make the character act and feel believable to you as well as the audience.

Now is the stage where your creativity can really help you express your idea to the Universe in more detail. You've started the process with your imagination. Now you can amplify your message to the Universe with your intention in the ways you like the most. Choose any of these, and do as many as you like. The method is not as important as finding a way of amplifying your message that is fun for you.

Words on paper – Write it up! Write your description of having what you are manifesting in a notebook. Use lots of adjectives and sensory words to describe the qualities that would make you feel the best. Describe your perfect day. Use present tense, as if you are already there. This is so important. Nothing is hypothetical. For instance, don't say, "If I could work from home, I'd…" You've already put in doubt if you used those beginning words. Instead, describe getting up in the morning, sitting in your comfy chair in your sweats, with your hot mug of creamy coffee at your side and your favorite music playing. You open your laptop and see a list of orders for your books have come in overnight. Use first person, present tense, as if you are describing what you **already have.**

As you write, feel it. Remember, emotional energy is the fuel! The more you can get deep enough into this description to feel excited, happy, grateful, and fulfilled, the more that message will shoot straight to the Universe for fulfillment. Go ahead and read it over when you're done, and let yourself really feel it as if you are already there.

Pictures on paper – Make a collage, either drawing, or using pictures from the Internet, magazines, or ads. Try to avoid using pictures of other people enjoying the scenario you want to be in. Remember, this is about you, not them. This is also referred to as a Vision Board. If you're the crafty type, you might really like this method! Enjoy finding pictures that represent what you are intending to manifest, and also pictures that evoke the happy, grateful feeling of having this scenario that you are bringing into being. As you choose the pictures, add them, and then look at them, see this as yours. Feel great about it! Feel excited and grateful.

Words out loud – You don't have to use any materials to do this exercise. If you enjoy daydreaming, or talking to yourself, go for it! Describe it to yourself in vivid detail in the words you use. This is good to do in the car if you're alone driving somewhere. Or, just at home alone is good too, because you can close your eyes if you want to. Talk about it in present tense, as if you already have this. Describe what you love about it, how great it feels to be there. For instance, if it's a new car, describe how it looks, and then how it feels to get inside, close the door, turn the key, and how it sounds when you're driving. How great does it feel to be in this nice new vehicle, designed to your specifications? What station will you play on the radio? Where are you driving? Remember to choose your words carefully so you aren't describing it as, "If I had a new car, I'd…" but instead, "In my new car, I am…"

As you describe it, remember to feel it too! Get into the scene emotionally, and know that the Universe is taking your order, fueled by your delight and gratitude. That's some high-test fuel right there!

When you finish this part, it's always great to say or think, "Thank you" to the Universe. Gratitude is powerful fuel, and a wonderful emotion to embrace as well.

EXPECTATION

Now you've done your imagining the outcome of what you're manifesting, and you've put your extra oomph into expressing that intention out to the Universe. This step is Expectation. Basically, it is the same as when you order something online, and then you are simply expecting it to arrive.

You don't usually sit around worrying if it will be delayed, or lost in transit, or broken when it arrives, do you? Wouldn't that be a waste of time? No, of course you don't. You just expect that package to arrive, excited to have this wonderful thing you ordered, and you are already imagining that it's in your hands. You might even say to yourself, "Oooh, I can't wait! It's coming soon, and I'm going to love this!" That's expectation.

Now, all you need to do is do the same thing with your goal. You've just gone to the effort of placing your order with The Universe. It's on its way! You can expect it to arrive soon. And so it is!

Did you know that the energy of expectation is at least as powerful, if not more powerful, than intention? That's because expectation is made of gratitude mixed with excitement. It's pure, positive emotional energy! So, just expect that your intentions will happen.

If you need help keeping your expectations positive (because, after all, negative expectations will produce negative results!), use affirmations that you can accept. See the last chapter for some examples.

Try this experiment: in the morning, say, "I'm going to receive a happy surprise today!" Then, go about your day with the expectation that any minute that happy surprise is going to happen. When it does (because if you are expecting it, it will!), say thank you to the Universe.

Remember: what we focus on grows stronger, and attracts more. So if we focus on gratitude, we will attract more things to be grateful for. If we focus on fear, we will attract more of what we're afraid of. What we focus on is our choice to make.

ACTION

Once you set your manifesting into motion, things are going to happen. This is the time to act on the opportunities and calls to action that you will find coming into your life that relate to what you are working to manifest.

Obviously, sitting around waiting for things to happen and doing nothing is not going to work. the Universe will bring you opportunities to move your goal forward. These will be new opportunities, or maybe ones that were there before, but you hadn't given them consideration until now. In any case, some ideas will grab your attention. That's the time to do something to move your goal ahead.

The Universe delivers your package in pieces, and sometimes it needs assembly. Follow up by putting the pieces together! Make the call, send the email, reach out to that new contact. Use a gap that just appeared in your day to write that article that you got an idea about, and submit it.

The Universe is your team, and you're the boss. That doesn't mean sitting still and letting your staff do all the work. It means getting involved in your part of things as they're progressing, to make sure that everything is on task.

If you're not sure what to do, ask for guidance. An easy way to do this is to simply take a moment to quiet your mind. Take some slow, deep breaths. Close your eyes. Then ask the question. Ask to be shown the next step. Then say, "Thank you" and expect that you'll know when it happens. You might get an idea when you're in the shower, or driving, or at a random time. Something might catch your attention or arrive in your Facebook feed. A person might approach you with a message. You'll receive what you need.

Don't wait around then! Follow up as soon as you can to keep the momentum going. Work as a team with the Universe and you'll find things happening quickly.

Stay excited and focused on expecting the very best at all times. Use your affirmations. Return to the first step, and review your intention-based expression to keep your positive emotions fueling your goal. The more you can come back to that emotional state of gratitude, excitement, anticipation, and keep the message clear, the faster you'll notice things will happen.

Summary of the Steps

To recap, the essential ingredients to manifesting are: Desire, Intention, Expectation, and Action. Each one is important, but how you do each step are products of your individual creative choices. Fuel each step with positive emotion. Keep an open mind and stay out of your own way. Notice the changes as they come and say thank you! Repeat the process often to keep energy flowing to fuel your goal.

THE SUPER FAST WAY: THE STAFF MEETING

I figured out this fast-track way to cover each step of the manifesting process, aloud, in a few minutes a day, or just a couple times a week. Since I'm not crafty, I just talk out loud. I do this in the car, usually, or else sometimes in the shower. I do it when I'm alone so no one will interrupt me, or give me weird looks or comments.

It starts with assuming that my life is a company. It's the Alice Company, because it's my company, and I'm Alice. (You can name your company anything you want). Of course, I hold the role of CEO of my life. In my company, I have an awesome staff, made up of only those who would want my absolute success and happiness, and be 100% committed to their jobs. My staff are comprised of my Guides and Angels. The Guides are my advisors. They give me guidance, advice, and ideas. The Angels are the team of coincidence-makers. They make things happen according to the very best possible outcome. (You can imagine any staff titles you want, as long as you have advisors and do-ers, so if you don't believe in angels you don't have to let that stop you from trying this.)

So, what does a CEO do? A CEO calls a meeting, of course. I call an **Executive Staff Meeting** of my team. In my mind, I sit at the head of the conference table, or behind a big, fancy desk in my awesome office. I always begin the meeting by thanking my hard working staff for the things that have been going great lately. For example, "I'd like to thank you all for bringing me that new Reiki client this week. She really loved her session and we had a great conversation too. And, great job on that store that purchased 65 copies of *A Moment for Teachers*. It's really exciting to know that my book's out there!" I keep going with the thanks until I've listed everything I'm grateful for that happened since our last meeting. Expressing gratitude to my team first helps me review all of the wonderful things occurring in my life, and I feel great! Good energy!

Next, I tell my team what the latest projects are,

and hand over assignments. For example, "Ok, Team, I've scheduled a Practical Reiki training for June. Angels, help fill those seats with the people who will benefit most from this training, and Guides, speak with the Guides of those people so their attention is drawn to the publicity about the class, or they find out about it in some way. Let me know what else I should do to help promote the class too." Does this sound familiar? I just put my Goal (Desire) out there by describing the outcome, and I used Intention to describe further what should be in there (people who will benefit most – remember that the goal should benefit others too?).

I also tell my team, "And, finally, I'm ready for any other nice surprises you have in store, and abundance from the unlimited channels available. Thanks, everyone! You are SO awesome and I know you're on the job!" What step is this? This is Expectation, of course, along with expressing excitement, confidence, and more gratitude.

Finally, I dismiss the meeting and stay present for guidance and noticing the things to add to the "Good Work" list for the next meeting. I'm left feeling positive, expecting the best, and also ready to take action when things start happening (such as responding to inquiry emails from prospective students, or putting out a flyer at a yoga studio near my office when I happen to notice it on my route). This exercise is completely sincere, fun, and positive.

Why this works:

Manifesting effectively requires essential ingredients. They are, in simplest form: **Gratitude, knowing and naming what you want** (specifically the end-results), and **expecting they are already coming into your life**. All pieces are present in this easy "Executive Staff Meeting."

I like keeping things simple. Not that there's anything wrong with vision boards, or a more complicated or longer process if that resonates with you. But basically, the creative force of the universe works by those simple steps combined with emotional energy. So, make sure that whatever method you choose includes them.

Happy Manifesting!!

RESOURCE CHARTS FOR INTENTION WORDING

It can be helpful to pay careful attention to the words you choose when setting your intention, or expressing it to the Universe. I created this resource to give you some ideas, and help you make positive wording choices.

Read the examples in the following charts, and adapt, revise, or create your own positive goal statements that fit what YOU want to manifest.

Love

Instead of this	Say this
Please bring me my soul mate. I will find someone soon.	My soul mate and I are being guided to each other now.
I want to find love.	The love in my heart shines out and attracts those with like vibrations.
I hope for a mate that's right for me.	I am ready to meet the person who compliments me completely.
I pray for love.	I am loving. I am worthy of love.
I need someone who will treat me right.	I am worthy of being valued completely, appreciated for who I am, and treated with love and respect. I am ready for this person to come into my life now.

Abundance

Instead of this	Say this
I need money. Please bring money now. I hope the money shows up! I'm praying for money every day. Money will come to me soon.	All my needs are being provided for. Abundance is flowing freely into my life. I am worthy of receiving what I need to be happy. Opportunities are coming into my life for me to use my skills to help others, and provide for my needs.
I want blessings and abundance in my life.	Blessings and abundance are flowing into my life from unlimited channels.
Please help me have enough money!	All of my debts are being taken care of, better than I can imagine them, for the best outcome for all concerned.
What will I do if I don't have enough money for XYZ?	Everything is working out for the best now. Answers and solutions are coming, clearly showing me the best possible outcome.

Career

Instead of this	Say this
I need a better job.	Opportunities are opening now for me to use the best of my skills and be appreciated.
I want a job working for XYZ company.	I'm ready to offer my skills and talents in the best position for me and those I can serve.
Please let me get this job!	I'm ready to follow the leads to connect me with the career that fits what I love to do, and offers the benefits that meet my needs.
I hate my job! It sucks! Get me out of this horrible situation! I will get a better job soon.	The best possible opportunity is being arranged for me now, where I can feel fulfilled in my work, and receive

A better job is in my future.	everything I need to live as I desire. I'm ready to respond to connections and requests that are being lined up for me now.

Life path

Instead of this	Say this
I need to find myself.	I'm ready to connect with the activities that make my heart sing. I am open to feeling the pull inside towards my calling.
Please help me find my purpose.	I have a purpose, to which I am beautifully suited, and I am ready to see the signs as they are coming to help me realize it fully.
I want a more fulfilling life.	I am here with my unique gifts, skills and knowledge, and ready for the opportunities to help.

	I am special, important, and worthy of creating and joyfully living the life I imagine. I am likeable and capable, and worthy of having a wonderful life.
I pray for happiness. I will be happier soon. Everything will be all right.	Unlimited joy, love, and opportunities are all around and flowing into my life now. Every day is getting better and better for me. I am ready to embrace every moment.

Who Are You and Why Have You Become So Strange?

How to deal with questions from skeptics, naysayers, and ourselves when we become more intuitive, spiritual, or both.

Alice Langholt
Reiki Master Teacher
Author of the Award-winning book
Practical Reiki: for balance, well-being, and vibrant health

DEDICATION

I dedicate this book to my husband, Evan, for being open-minded enough to accept me, support me, and ultimately, brag about me, even when the things I did seemed strange.

CONTENTS

What is Weird?	110
What Happens When Something is Weird?	114
What Happens When Someone Rejects You	118
How to Encourage a Shift	126
What to do When People are Confused by You	131
How to Decide if Someone (or We) Are Intuitive or Crazy	136
Conclusion	142

WHAT IS WEIRD?

It may sound like a silly, or simplistic question to ask, "What is weird?" However, think about it. If you point at something and say, "This is normal. That is weird," will everyone agree with you? Is there a single standard for weirdness or normalcy? If someone behaves in a way that's usual for him, does that make it usual for you, or universally normal? Is there a universal standard for normal?

If Joe gets up every morning at 5 am to meditate, exercise, and routinely has a hard-boiled egg for breakfast, and Sarah gets up at 9 am, drinks coffee, and skips breakfast, which of them is "weird"? Would Joe think it's weird not to get up early, or would Sarah think it's weird to get up at 5 am? Perhaps both would agree that no one holds a patent on "normal" and it's possible for different things to be "normal" even if it the behavior is not normal for someone else.

So, what is weird?

To throw the question back to you, what do **you** think is weird? Your answer would likely describe weird as something that is so far outside the realm of your own personal reality that it causes a conflict with that idea.

Weird and ordinary are relative terms. They are both subjective. Other cultures' norms seem weird to us, while ours are weird to them. Animal behavior would be weird if we did it, but ordinary for the animal to do what they do naturally. **Whatever we get used to doing becomes ordinary for us**, and, guess what, that "ordinary" can change if we change our habits.

For instance, if it became routine for you to smoke a cigarette after lunch, then that would be your habit. It would be part of your ordinary, day-to-day life. But, if you decided to quit smoking, it would feel "weird" or out of the ordinary to abstain from your post-lunch smoke. You'd likely look for something else to take the place of that activity to create a new habit. Change feels confusing. But, you can decide to change your behavior, and create a new "normal" for you, which will eventually feel comfortable. Once you got used to not smoking, then considering smoking again would feel weird. You might even feel grossed-out or resentful of others who smoke once you define yourself as a non-smoker.

There are degrees of weirdness, too. Something outside of our own experience or understanding could be classified as:

~**interesting** – in that it's different, but not an unpleasant idea, possibly even an idea that we would like to try.

~**odd** – in that we would need to consider it, perhaps research more, before thinking about trying it, if we would even want to.

~**strange** – in that it's outside of our ordinary reality, unexpected, and confusing to us, possibly even enough to laugh about.

~**bizarre** – in that it's so foreign to us that we're baffled by it, and likely uncomfortable.

~**crazy** – in that we can't understand it, and might even find it frightening or repulsive on some level.

What we learn here is that "weird" is a relative term, and evokes different reactions, ranging from curiosity to revulsion. It always exists relative to our own idea of reality- our own sense of normalcy- which is based on our experience, culture, and environment.

Imagine a circle around you and everything you

feel is "regular, ordinary, or normal." What's outside of that circle is what you would call "weird," as well as all of the level categories above. These labels are applied by you, relative to how close or far away they are to your own acceptance of normal. The farther away the designations are, the less likely you are to relate to them, or to be interested in trying them.

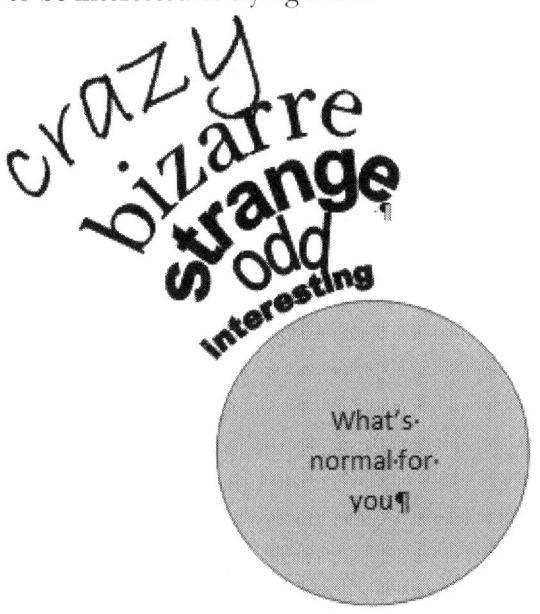

crazy bizarre strange odd interesting

What's normal for you

This ebook is intended to try to help the reader gain perspective on themselves in relation to their own past, themselves in relation to the state and expectations of friends and family, and provide tools to use when conflicts arise.

WHAT HAPPENS WHEN SOMETHING IS WEIRD?

When a person is exposed to something outside of their circle of "normal," the person needs to decide where that idea fits on the spectrum of "weird." That decision may be easy, or may be very difficult, depending on the person's initial reaction.

The new idea may be interesting – meaning that the person is willing to explore it, maybe try it out to see if it's effective, useful, or enlightening. That's the "try it!" stage. People are generally willing to try something that fits into this category.

Imagine that you are exposed to a new idea

that seems appealing to you. You might decide to learn more about it, from a teacher, or from reading, or taking a video lesson. You step a little bit outside your comfort level to try it. Maybe it works, and you like it! You decide to do it some more. You decide to practice this new thing. You incorporate this into your routine. Pretty soon, this new idea moves inside your circle of "normal" and is no longer weird.

That's called a paradigm shift. It means that you have changed your mind about something, and accepted it.

Paradigm shifts follow a process. Here are the stages of a paradigm shift:

~Disbelief – This is the first stage. It's when you think, "What? No way can that be real!" This is a common reaction to supernatural concepts such as psychic abilities, paranormal events, and spiritual experiences. Some people never get beyond this stage.

> If a person decides that the idea is interesting and harmless enough to step outside their comfort zone and explore, that person may be able to get to the next stage, Testing.

~Testing – At this stage, you try the new idea out. You might research it to learn more. You might try the new skill for yourself and see what happens. If something conclusive happens, like it works, or you can do it, you might decide that the idea is, in fact, real. More likely, however, you might need to repeat the testing process over and over until your results are consistent enough for you to accept the concept as real. It will then shift to the next stage, Acceptance, when it moves inside your circle. This is where the paradigm shift happens.

Here is an example. Up until my late 30's, I had never heard of Reiki. (Reiki is an energy healing technique that originated in Japan, in which one uses intention to balance life force energy to release stress, relieve pain, and speed healing.) This invisible healing technique seemed strange and new to me, and the concept was outside the realm of my personal experience up to that point. I was curious, however, and was very interested in experiencing something outside of my usual 5-sense limitations. So, I signed up for a Reiki class. The information alone, however, was not enough for me to believe it was real, or that I was able to do it. I needed more.

What I needed was to **experience** the energy for myself – to actually **feel** it somehow. Not only once, but I needed to feel it **every time** I tried to activate it. I needed to trust in my own experience, and it had to be consistent for me in order for me to trust in my ability to do Reiki. I needed to have enough practice and feedback to shift me from **Testing** to **Acceptance.**

~**Acceptance** – This stage is when you believe that the new idea is real, so it is no longer "weird," but you accept it as "normal" and it moves inside your circle. Once I accepted that Reiki is real, and I can do it, I was fascinated with Reiki! I needed to learn more, and see how much I could grow in my ability. I was very motivated to keep practicing and learning from my own experiences. This was a very big shift in my life.

Whether a person is willing to take the first step away from the initial Disbelief stage to the Testing stage is very individual. No one can "make" another person believe something. No one can force a person into a paradigm shift. The shifting has to be done by the individual, and has to be accepted by that person when that person is willing. We'll discuss this further in the next chapter.

WHAT HAPPENS WHEN SOMEONE REJECTS YOU?

When a person has had a paradigm shift, and now includes something previously thought of as "weird" in his "normal" circle, it can cause a new division between him and his friends and family, who may still have that new concept outside of their "normal" circles.

To put it simply, those who know us might think that we're suddenly weird, or embracing a foreign concept. They may think we've changed, which could be true, or that we're suddenly harder to relate to than we used to be, due to this new development.

That can bring about discomfort, at least, or

even permanent division, in more extreme cases where the family member or friend can no longer accept us with our new belief or practice. Many times, people are comfortable with their personal understanding of reality, and stepping outside of that is frightening to them. Fear is a powerful limitation, and trying something new can be legitimately scary for people. Stepping into unknown realms can be scary for most people, depending on what they perceive might result. Perhaps a new experience would challenge what they had believed before. Seeing a family member or friend suddenly embracing a new idea which conflicts with their sense of reality causes tension which can extend to the relationship itself.

Here are some of the ways people tend to deal with the issue that arises when their reality conflicts with someone else's:

Hide – This person will be "in the closet" about his or her new idea, skill, or belief, in order to avoid conflict. The person decides that it's simply not worth it to argue with those who are not ready to even entertain the new idea due to whatever is keeping them in their own circle. I know many people who secretly practice Reiki, or don't tell people that they do card readings, or have other intuitive abilities. They do this because they know that their family would not accept this, and would reject them if they knew.

When I first started practicing Reiki professionally, I was shy about mentioning it around people that knew me from my other career as a Jewish Educator. I thought these people would think that I'm weird, or talk about me behind my back. I was afraid of being uncomfortable. In fact, when I started learning Reiki, even my husband thought that it was fake, and that I was wasting my time. I wasn't confident enough yet to deal with the confusion of my family, friends, and acquaintances yet, so I basically kept quiet about it.

I remember the first time I wrote "Reiki Master" as my job title on one of my children's school forms. It was very liberating! It was a big shift for me to "go public" with it, and decide that I didn't care what people thought about it anymore. It took courage.

Become Defensive – People who are challenged about the new belief might feel defensive in trying to explain why they believe it is real. They will tell their story, explain how they learned it, explain why it's real, what they felt, all in attempt to convince the skeptical confronter that the new belief is worth accepting. This is an uncomfortable feeling, because often the person feels as if he is defending his very integrity, and possibly sanity, to those who are now questioning it. The family member or friend is now looking at the person as if he, by association with the "weird" belief that is outside of their "normal" circle, is also "weird." That puts the person in the position of defending himself, as well as what he believes.

Attempt to educate, convince others to grow – The person may now try to teach, offer materials such as studies, statistics, or use other persuasive techniques to get their friends or family to step toward interest or curiosity, rather than denial of this new paradigm. If the people are willing to listen, this could be helpful. If not, it can become an argument, or frustrating process. After a number of unsuccessful attempts, the person may give up and try something else on the list. It really depends on the willingness of the people outside this paradigm to entertain the notion, and perhaps learn more about it.

Try to "prove" that the belief is real – This is a more intense step than the attempt to educate mentioned above. This involves offering an experience, or demonstration, in hopes of shifting the outsider from denial to interest.

I have given many Reiki demonstrations, and challenge the recipient to describe "what's different" in order for him to admit and describe the sensations of the Reiki energy. Remember – **experience is powerful**. If I can help a person experience Reiki energy, he will be much more likely to want to move to the "testing" phase and learn more. I've already gotten inside that person's circle.

I have often compared Reiki to a spiritual experience. It is easier to share Reiki with someone than it is to share a spiritual experience. That's because it is possible to help a person feel Reiki, or learn Reiki and use it themselves. In contrast, you can tell a person about your spiritual experience, but you can't give that experience to him or her. You can't "make" that person have the same experience. In either case, however, the person needs to be willing to try in order to have an experience that might help him step outside of his "normal circle."

Isolation – If you've tried to show people the new concept and were rejected, or you are convinced that the people in your life would not accept you nor your new belief or skill, it may make you want to isolate yourself. You don't feel that you fit in any longer with the crowd that you used to associate with, and you don't have new peers to talk to who accept your new ideas. This can be depressing in some cases. It's not a great solution, but can be temporarily needed.

When I first started getting into Reiki, and my husband thought it was weird, I didn't have any friends who practiced Reiki. I didn't have anyone to talk to about it. I felt alone, because when I had tried to talk about it with anyone in my family, they didn't understand and weren't very interested, either. It was frustrating. I went through a period of isolation, just practicing on my own. It didn't take long, however, for me to seek out others to talk with, because isolation was uncomfortable for me, and because I knew that in order to learn more, I needed people who had Reiki inside their "normal circle," and were willing to discuss it with me.

Find a group of people with common beliefs – Finding a community, a tribe, a group, or at least one peer to discuss our new belief, skill, or understanding with is very helpful. It's really a relief to have people to talk to! Usually, those we find will be just as eager to talk about it as we are. Community brings about a feeling of support, and acceptance that we have been craving if it is not found within our circle of family and friends.

I found people by starting a blog, joining discussion groups, and seeking out other Reiki practitioners in my community. I also approached two friends and asked them if they'd be willing to help me practice distance healing, and provide feedback. You might find Meetups in your area for those interested in your new topic, and instantly there's a community for you. There are groups on Facebook, Yahoo, Reddit, and many other online locations that will accept you and help you feel connected.

Doubt ourselves, reassess, try to fit in with our old belief system – There might be a period of stepping back if we are faced with people who don't understand our new paradigm and interest. This is especially true if we "stay in the closet" about the shift. We might decide it isn't worth it to continue, because of the conflicts and potential conflicts that could happen. We might try to go back to our old life before our shift happened. We might even doubt that the experience was that powerful or real, and leave it behind entirely. On the surface, it might seem easier to do this.

However, ultimately, a person who does this may end up feeling like an imposter as the new paradigm, now ignored, is still pulling his or her thoughts. The person may feel like something is missing. It is hard to go back to who you were before you had a period of enlightenment. Things tend to feel different, and a little fake. This option is often temporary.

I've read many books in which a person who learned or discovered energy healing tried to ignore it, and went back to his life before, just to find his life fell apart soon after, leaving him no option but to embrace the gift. One such book is called *Whose Hands Are These?* and I recommend it highly.

HOW TO ENCOURAGE A SHIFT

To expand your horizons and learn something new, these things need to happen. You can know these steps for yourself, and take them, or you can encourage others to do these steps. These are the ingredients that are basic to a paradigm shift. I broke them down into three steps:

Be open – No one expects you to believe something without experiencing it. Skeptical is fine, as long as it includes a willingness to experiment. The best attitude is described by, "I don't know, but I'll try." This is an experimental attitude.

Think of yourself as a scientist, about to try an experiment. If you go into the experiment expecting it to fail, chances are that you will skew the results. A scientist must go into the experiment open-minded and inquisitive, ready to observe rather than judge any results while the experiment is taking place. During this process the scientist is interested in recording data rather than analyzing it. Try the new thing, and observe what happens – these are the essential parts of this open-minded step.

Be willing to allow your experience to teach you your "Truth." – This is part of the open-minded bit, because in order to make a shift, a person needs to be willing to accept a result that might be different from expected. Releasing expectations allows one to be open-minded enough to notice something new or different. Then, the testing phase can happen as much as needed.

This is needed because in order for a person to be able to shift to a new paradigm, the person needs to be able to trust himself. He needs to step outside of the idea that only an "expert" has the ultimate knowledge or understanding of how things are. The person needs to be able to question the authority of sources out there, and trust his own experience. Sometimes that, in itself, requires a powerful shift.

There are websites pro and con for most things, and all of them claim to be "true." Some will refute the legitimacy of an idea, and others will proclaim the idea to be real. It's important for individuals to be able to accept, or even entertain, the authority of their own experience in order to be open-minded enough to give something new a try.

Funny story – When I started offering distance Reiki healings, my husband was very skeptical, even negative, about me doing that. He told me this couldn't be real, and to stop wasting my time. I was in a place where I needed to keep experimenting with Reiki so I could learn for myself what the power of it was, and I was also getting some really interesting results. So, I kept offering distance Reiki sessions with quiet confidence, and basically ignored my husband's scoffing.

Then, I started getting paid for distance healing sessions. This happened a few times. When I told my husband, he was surprised, at first. Then, after it happened a few times, he became curious. He got to a place in himself where his curiosity outweighed his denial. He asked me to teach him Reiki so he could experience it for himself. I did, he felt it, and he started respecting my Reiki practice.

Try, observe, repeat until you believe it's true. This is the process of "testing" that must happen as many times as you need to do it until you are convinced that the new belief either works for you, or doesn't. Either answer is all right! Neither answer is wrong, if you have tested it with an open mind.

When I started giving distance Reiki attunements, I first attuned 12 people free of charge, with the only requirement being that these people give me feedback to indicate if they could feel the energy, and it was working for them. I told myself that if it didn't work **even once**, I would quit doing Reiki. I needed to have consistent results in order to feel comfortable charging for these services. I knew that I was not comfortable offering Reiki professionally if sometimes I was going to be afraid it wouldn't work. I needed Reiki to be dependable, with positive feedback, so that I could tell someone relying on me that it would work. I'm not trying to say, "Just believe me." Rather, I wanted to be able to say, "Try it and you'll see for yourself." I think that is much more powerful of a statement, as well as freeing. First, however, I needed to be certain that it was true. Offering to teach a dozen students gave me the opportunity to prove for myself that distance attunements work, in order for me to then state with confidence that I could show others.

WHAT TO DO WHEN PEOPLE ARE CONFUSED BY YOU

If you have shifted to a new paradigm, and those around you are confused or having difficulty understanding or accepting you, here are a few suggestions for how to handle the situation:

Have Quiet Confidence – This means just keep doing what you need to. Practice, learn, connect with like-minded souls. Continue despite what others are saying, until such a time when they are interested enough to let you share. You will gain the advantage of more experience, knowledge, and finer-honed skills in the process, along with more results from your work. You also don't have to engage in any debates. You're just learning for yourself here.

This is what I did when my husband thought I was doing something that was fake, or a waste of time. I knew that something was happening, and he wasn't ready to listen. So, I kept working at it, kept learning, despite his attitude. Eventually, the results I was getting got his attention, and he became willing to ask me about it.

If the person is open, offer to demonstrate – Once the person is open enough to be willing to listen, offer to give the person the chance to **experience** what you do in some way. Demonstrate, explain, show results. Do whatever you can to help the person feel or experience what you do. This helps a person learn that experience is powerful! Perhaps the person will be willing to take the next step toward a paradigm shift.

If the person isn't, it's not your problem. – This is pretty important. Be willing to not take it personally if the person rejects what you believe, or even can't talk with you, because he is not able to make the shift from denial. If this happens, go back to **quiet confidence.** You don't have to argue, discuss, or try to persuade the person, and it wouldn't work anyway. You know that what you're doing is working, or at least fascinating to you. Keep doing it, but don't bother pushing someone who isn't ready.

Allow the results to speak for themselves. – Eventually, you will get to a place where you are getting powerful and consistent results from your work. The more you do, the more people who previously were doubtful or uninterested will become curious or respectful of the new information. Meanwhile, you will be doing something good for people who want and need your services, as well as reinforcing for yourself that what you are doing is valid.

Your confidence will increase the more you practice, and get results. So, keep doing that. There are people who need, and want, what you can offer. So, focus on those people rather than others who are not ready. Regardless of whether the others will ever be ready or not, you're doing work that matters.

Create your elevator speech and craft different versions for different audiences. – Being able to talk about what you do in a way that others can understand is a big key to helping people shift towards you. In order to do that, you need to create some working definitions of what you do. These definitions must meet the needs of who is asking. For instance, I have different ways of explaining Reiki to children than I have for explaining to doctors, other holistic practitioners, people new to the concept of energy healing, and other Reiki practitioners. That's because each of these populations has a different experience set and comes with a certain vocabulary.

For kids, I say, "Reiki is a warm energy that feels good, and helps you feel better when something is wrong." Kids can relate to the need to feel better, and feeling good. They are comfortable with that explanation.

For people who aren't familiar with Reiki at all, I start with, "Reiki is an energy healing method for pain relief, stress, relief, and better health." This definition includes three conditions that the average person can relate to, and benefits.

For doctors, I might mention that Reiki works with the human biofield, and encourages stress relief. Since stress increases pain and impedes healing, Reiki helps by producing a relaxing effect, which then results in reduction of pain and easier healing.

Other Reiki practitioners usually were trained in the more traditional approach to Reiki than what I teach. I would talk to those people about the differences between Practical Reiki (the method I teach) and Usui Reiki (the traditional method).

So, you can see that by having different short definitions geared to meet the needs of different people who might ask, I am speaking about Reiki in a way that's relatable to each, as it meets the person where he or she is at, and uses words that are in the experience set of that person. This practice helps a person feel comfortable, and may encourage the person to be willing to step forward to learn more.

HOW TO DECIDE IF SOMEONE IS (OR WE ARE) INTUITIVE OR CRAZY

Sometimes, we will encounter people who practice or proclaim truths that feel very uncomfortable to us. We may wonder if a person is delusional or having hallucinations. We may question that person's credibility. Then we might doubt ourselves for wondering, reasoning that what we do is, and was once, considered crazy too. Our boundaries between intuitive and crazy come into question, leaving us confused.

I understand. I've been there. I have, many times, exhibited at psychic fairs and wellness expos. At every one, I have noticed people that are far on the outside of what I have experienced.

These people seem to teeter on the edge of what seems rational in my own mind. It has left me wondering how far "reality" goes, and where the line for "crazy" begins. It's even caused me to doubt my own ability to discern. I've chided myself for being limited, and closed-minded, even though I have a wider range of experience than many people I know.

Here are some tips for when these moments happen to you:

Be aware of what behaviors are outside of your "normal" boundary. When you observe something that causes you to feel uncomfortable, doubtful, or strange, ask yourself what about this idea or behavior is bothering you. If it's just that you haven't experienced it, but it may be possible, then note that for yourself. Do your best to step outside of judgement and observe the qualities that strike you as questionable. You want to get ready to assess these qualities against your own beliefs in as rational a way as you are able.

Ask yourself about the source of your discomfort. Is it fear? Humans have a natural tendency to fear what is foreign or unknown. Are you fearing something because you haven't had experience with it? Is your fear rational? These are questions to start with. What makes you uncomfortable about this person or idea? Your answer to these questions will be helpful.

Assess: Does this idea belong in my "I don't know file"? There are many things that we do not know, but that doesn't make them not real. I have a mental "I don't know file" which is where I mentally file new ideas that I do not yet have experience enough to judge. I consider these ideas possible, but I put them on the back burner until I have had the chance to test them for myself.

Among the things in my "I don't know file" are creatures such as dragons, fairies, and trolls. I might have previously dismissed these as silly ideas. However, I have colleagues who I respect, that have had experience with each of these mythical creatures. That leads me to reserve judgement until such a time as I might have an encounter with any of these beings. I'm open to doing so, and curious about the idea. Whenever that might happen, the concept will then easily move from my "I don't know file" into my "experienced it file" so I can do further testing.

I used to have angels in my "I don't know file." After much reaching out and testing, based on many techniques I read about in Amy Oscar's book, *Sea of Miracles*, I had enough experience with angels to verify for myself that angels are real, and here to help us every day. If you are wondering about angels, I encourage you to read Amy's book. It changed my life.

Ask yourself key questions. There are three key questions to ask yourself if we are wondering if someone's beliefs are crazy or not.

The first is, **"Is this belief causing harm to anyone?"** Is the person's behavior harming themselves or others? If so, it would be prudent to take steps to get that person help. A person's beliefs should not cause harm. Any beliefs that are causing a person to be afraid, or dangerous, are indications of mental illness. By the way, you can use this question for yourself too, if needed. If you are hearing a voice, or voices, that are telling you to self-harm or harm others, please seek help.

The second is, **"How is this person handling the rest of his/her life?"** My husband worked for many years in the mental health field. He used to tell me that people have the right to be crazy, or believe whatever they want, as long as they are eating, sleeping, and bathing, and are not harming themselves or others. That's an important perspective. We are not where others are, and whether or not we will ever get there, it's important to allow someone who is not harmful to believe what they choose to believe.

The third is, **"Does this person seem otherwise grounded?"** This means, does the person seem to be rooted in reality besides having a belief that is challenging your own? If the answer is, "yes" then you can step back and put the person's idea into your "I don't know file" or not.

Once, I was at a psychic fair, as a vendor. I was in my booth, talking with visitors about Reiki. One woman approached my booth and engaged me in conversation. She kept pausing, however, to consult her "guides" at many times while we were speaking. It bothered me, because I felt that her doing this was taking her away from our conversation, and confusing me. It seemed to me that this practice of constantly consulting her "guides" was removing her from being present for a basic conversation with me. There's a time and place for checking in with higher guidance, and mundane conversations don't seem to be times where this sort of in-depth introspection is needed.

My personal "I don't know file" comes in handy. It helps me be open minded about new ideas. There isn't a lot that falls outside of the realm of that file. However, the above are ways in which I have chosen to filter my own responses to the new ideas in my day to day encounters.

CONCLUSION

Growing, ascending, and shifting are all parts of a complicated process. Without them, however, we would be stagnant, feel stuck, and miss out on a lot of new learning. This lifetime is an opportunity to learn all we can. It's impossible to learn if a person feels that he knows everything. There has to be a measure of humility and open-mindedness in a person in order for him to grow, learn, and expand.

As humans, if we don't grow, we are stuck where we are. We may feel like victims of our own circumstances, but these limitations are belief systems only! What we believe becomes our reality. Choosing to be open-minded, to learn from experience, and to be willing to entertain new ideas is the best part of being human.

My advice is: learn everything you can. Be willing to explore, and let your experience teach you your Truth. You can always give up old Truths for new ones. You can always grow into new discoveries, if you give yourself the chance to experiment.

That doesn't mean that everything is true. But it also doesn't mean that everything that you haven't yet experienced is false. I hope that this ebook has helped you understand the process of testing new ideas, dealing with those who are not ready, and knowing when you are, or are not, ready to progress.

If there's anything I can do to help you, please contact me via ReikiAwakeningAcademy.com and I'll do my best to help.

ABOUT THE AUTHOR

Alice Langholt is a Reiki Master Teacher, the Executive Director of Reiki Awakening Academy School of Intuitive Development (ReikiAwakeningAcademy.com), and the founder of Practical Reiki, a strong, simple Reiki energy healing method.

Alice is the author of the award-winning book, *Practical Reiki for balance, well-being, and vibrant health, A guide to a strong, revolutionary energy healing method*, and *The Practical Reiki Companion* workbook, as well as three apps, the *A Moment for Me 365 Day Self Care Calendar for Busy People*, and other books in the A Moment for Me series. (AMoment4Me.com).

She's passionate about finding and teaching simple approaches to strengthening intuition and achieving holistic balance.

Alice lives with her husband and their four children in Gaithersburg, Maryland.

She teaches Practical Reiki and other holistic topics, and offers workshops on 30 second methods of self-care online and in the Washington, DC area.

Contact Alice by email at Alice@AliceLangholt.com

Made in the USA
Lexington, KY
01 March 2019